Realistic Art: How To Draw Jesus

Art Lessons: How to Draw a Portrait of Jesus

How to Draw Jesus

By : Gala Publication

2

Published By :

Gala Publication

© Copyright 2015 – Gala Publication

ISBN-13: **978-1522801030**
ISBN-10: **1522801030**

Table of Contents

Table of Contents

BABY JESUS

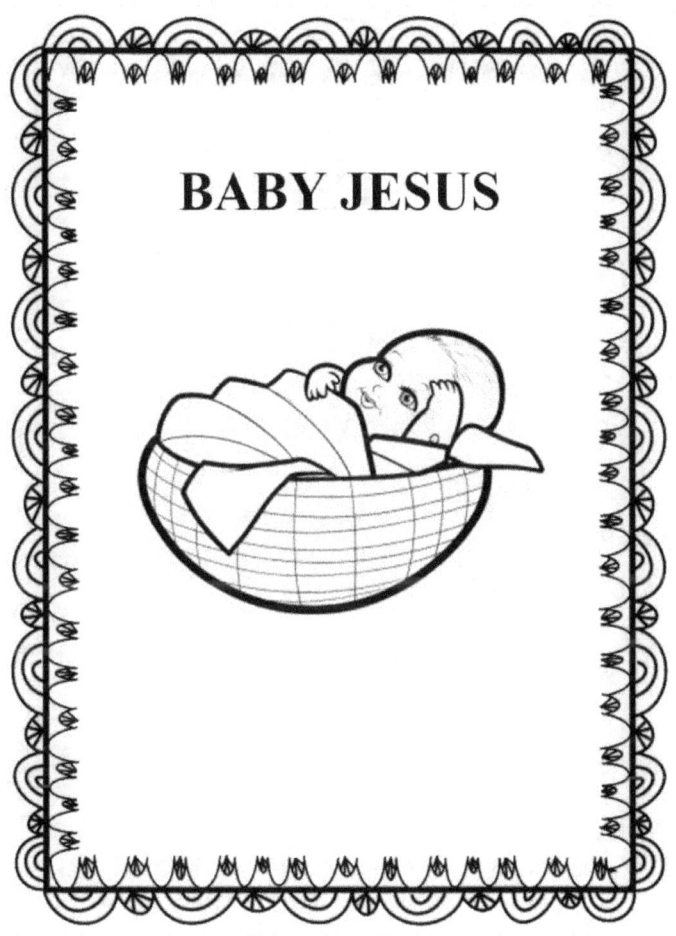

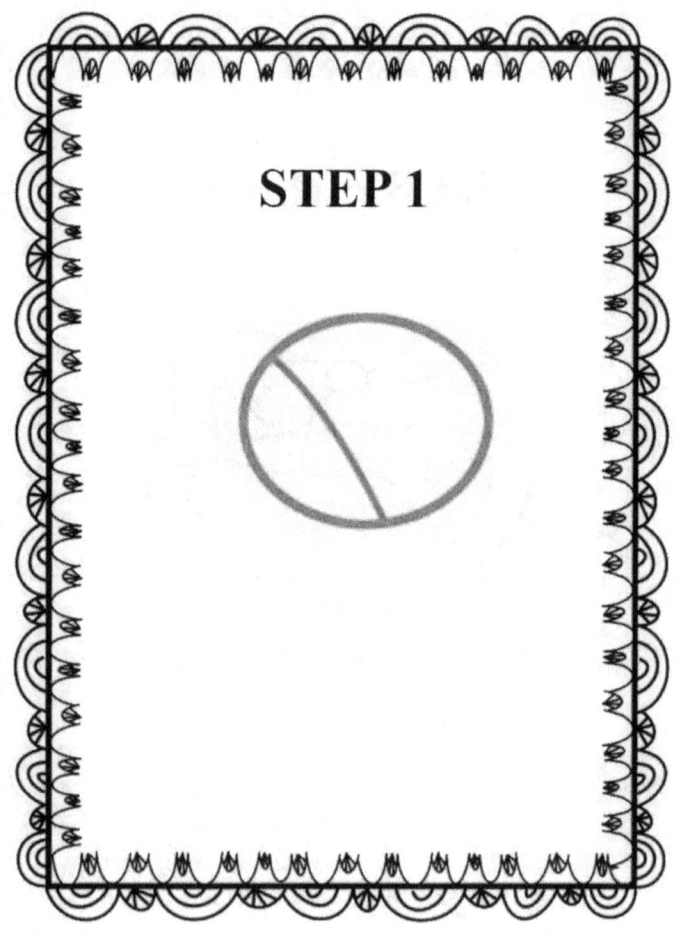

STEP 1

STEP 2

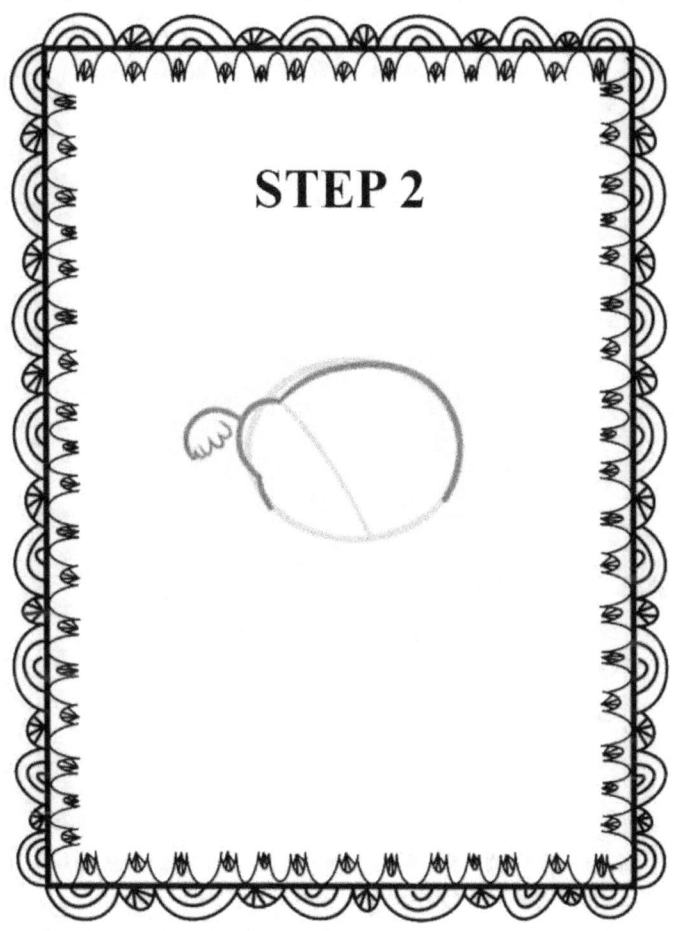

STEP 3

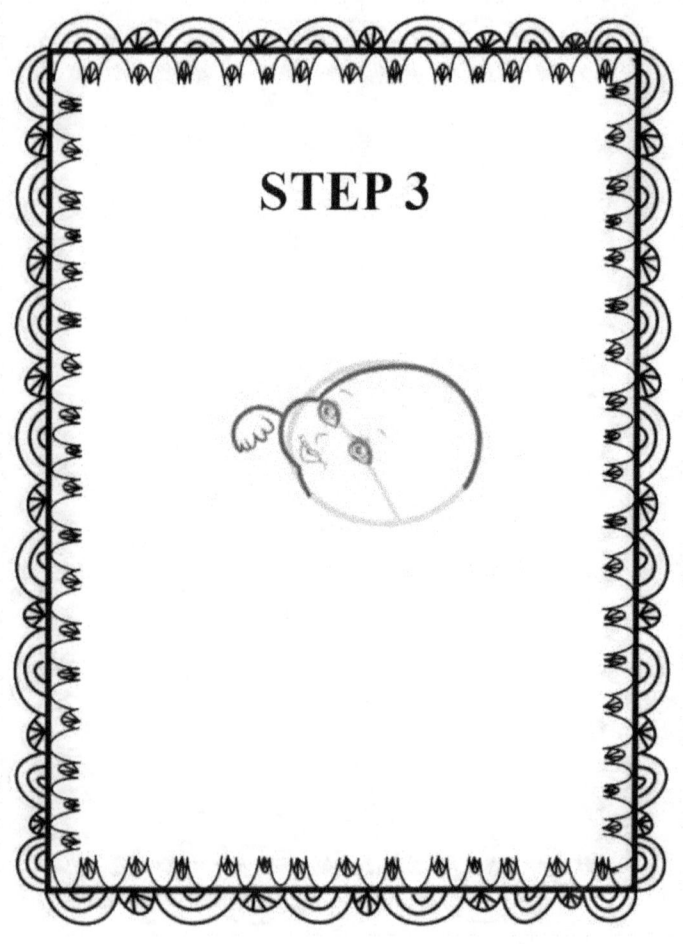

STEP 4

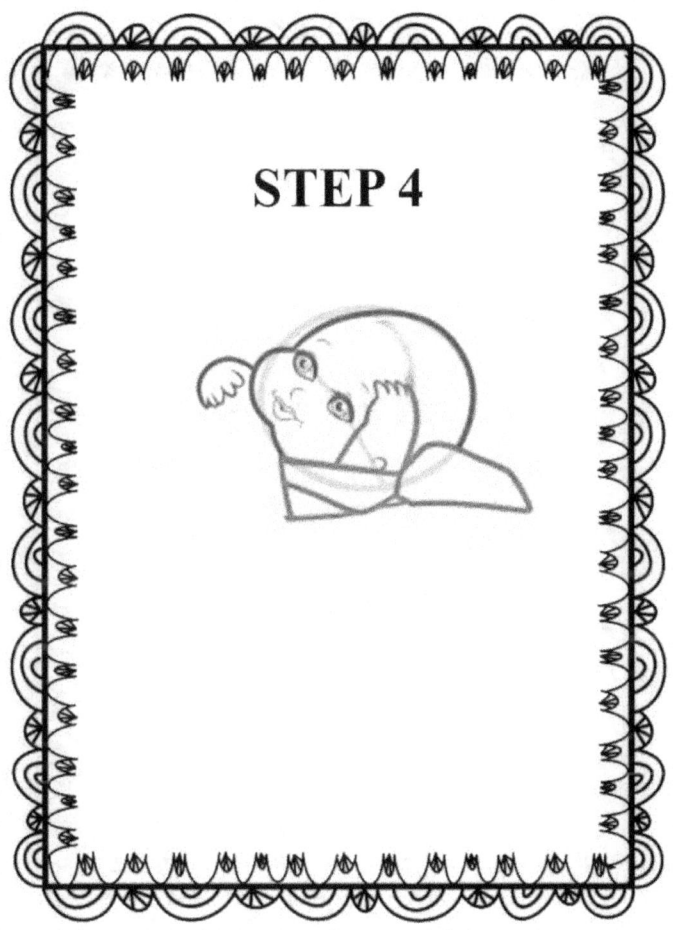

STEP 5

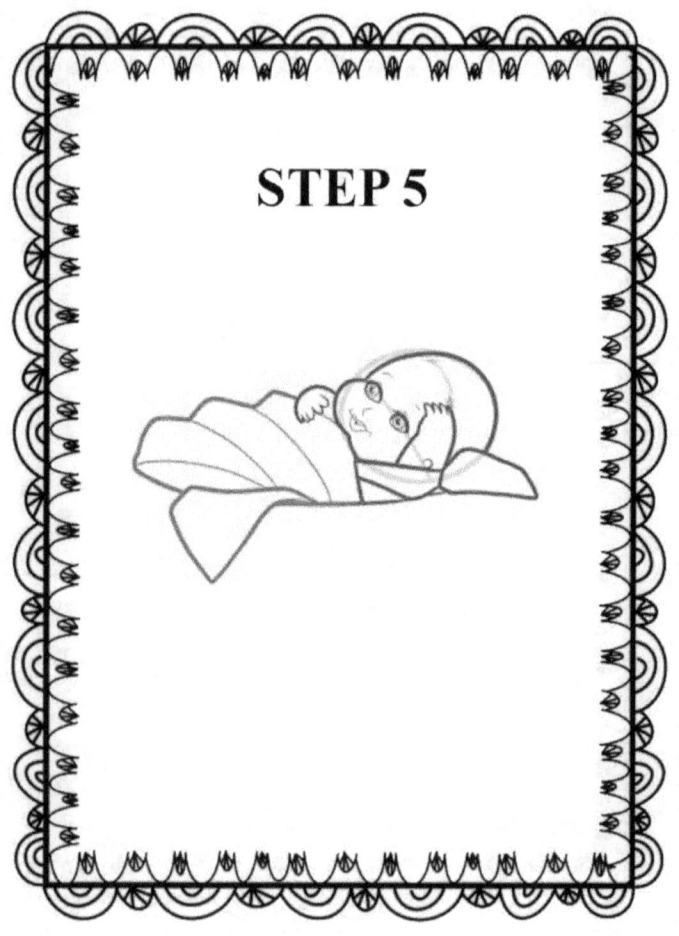

STEP 6

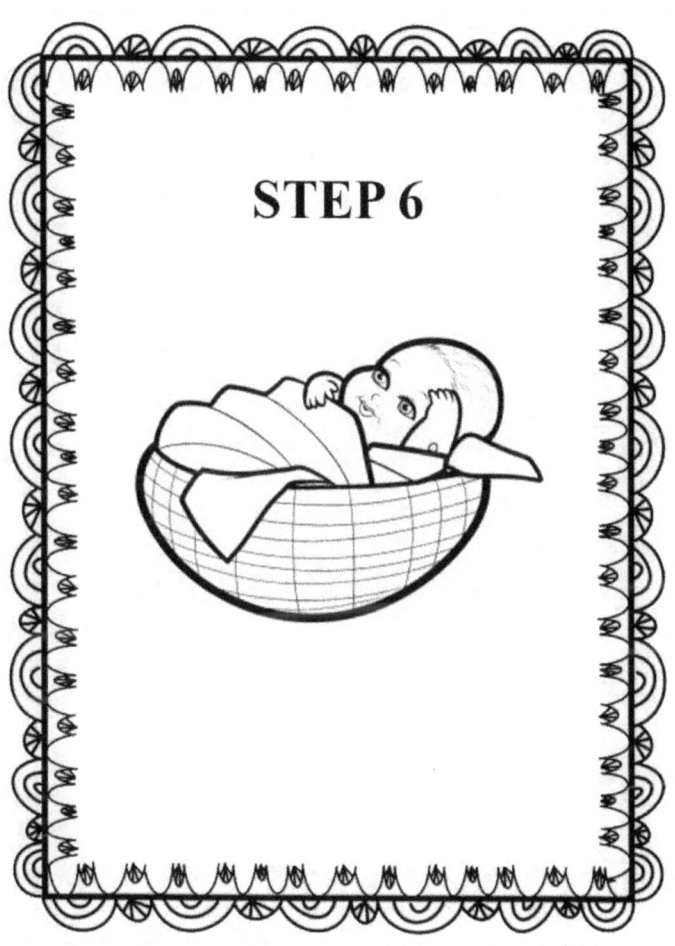

CROSS JESUS

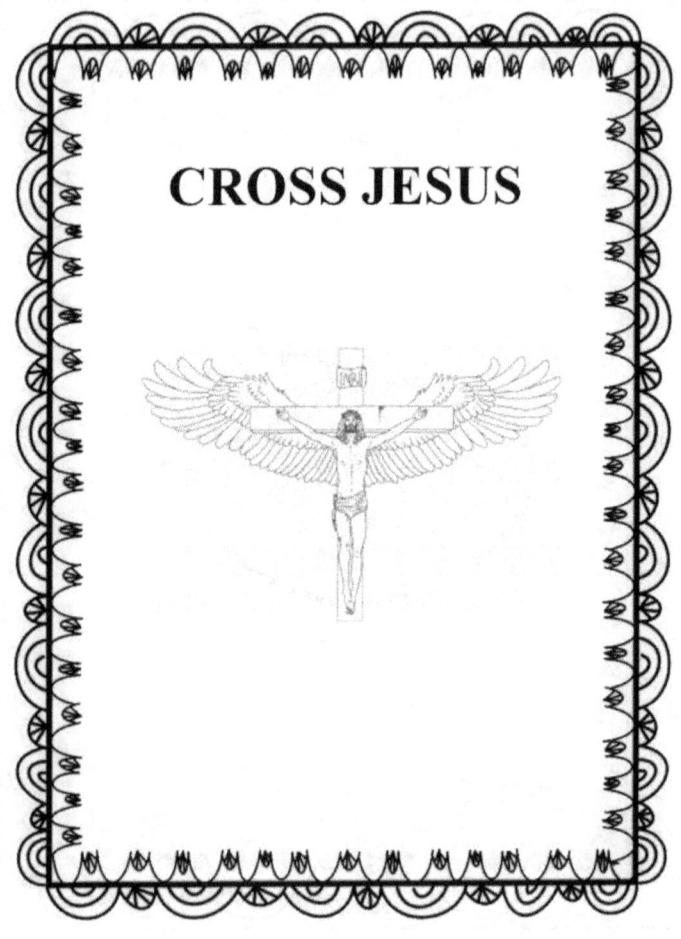

STEP 1

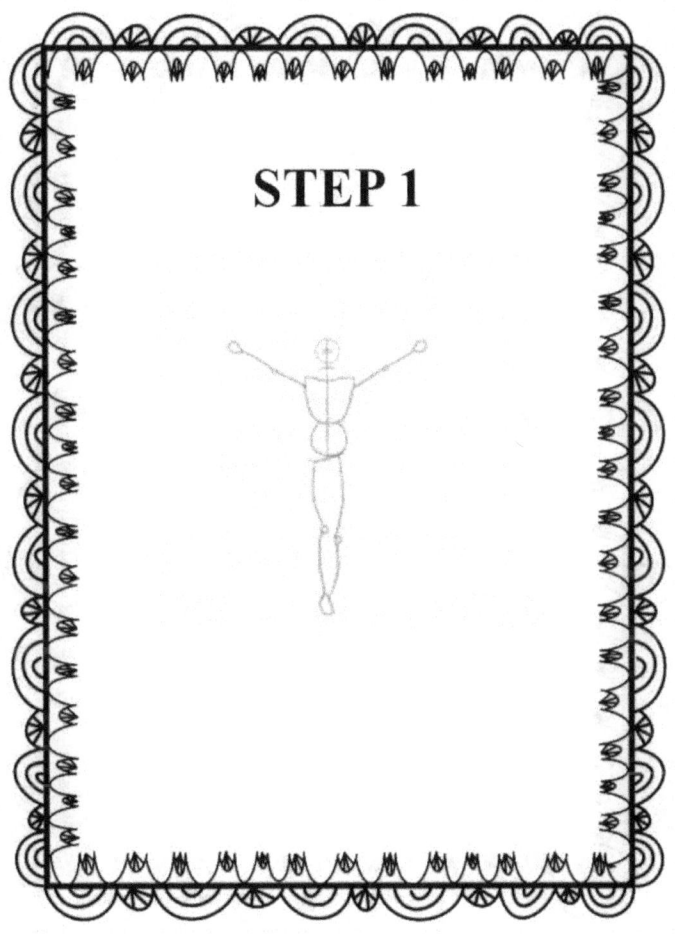

STEP 2

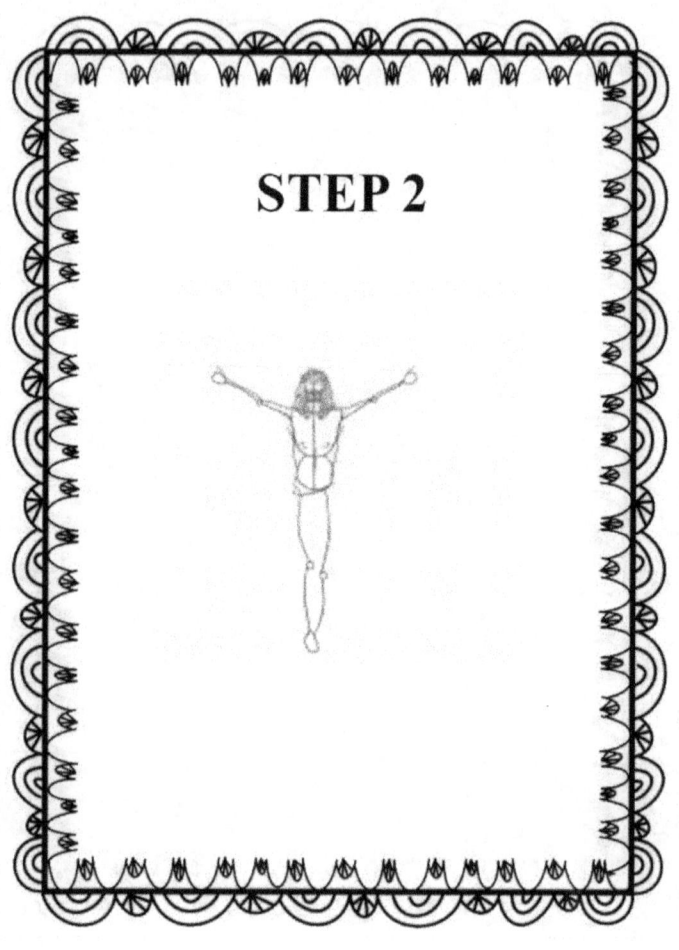

STEP 3

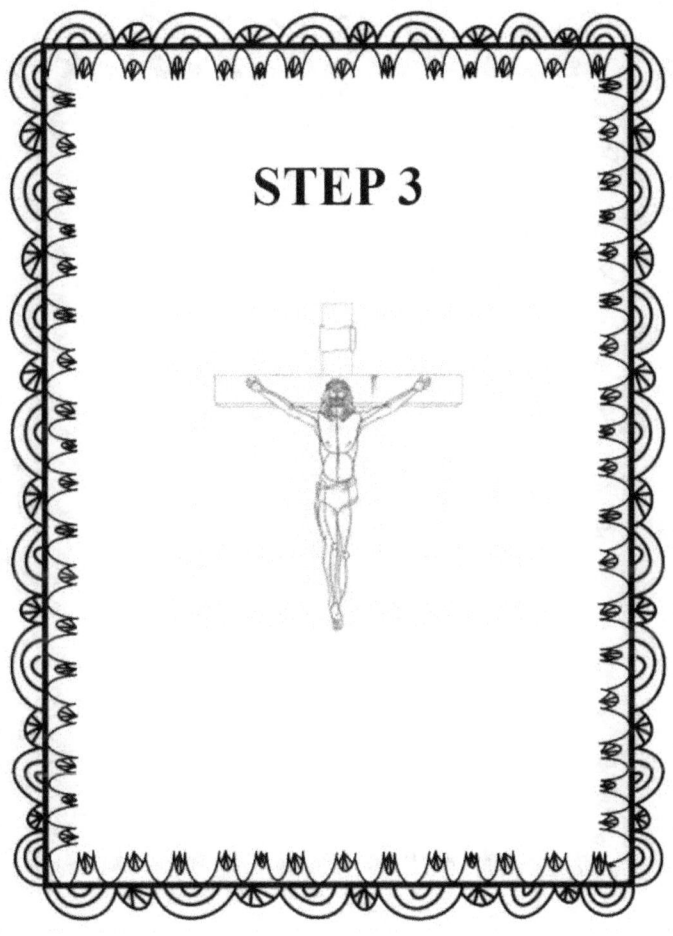

STEP 4

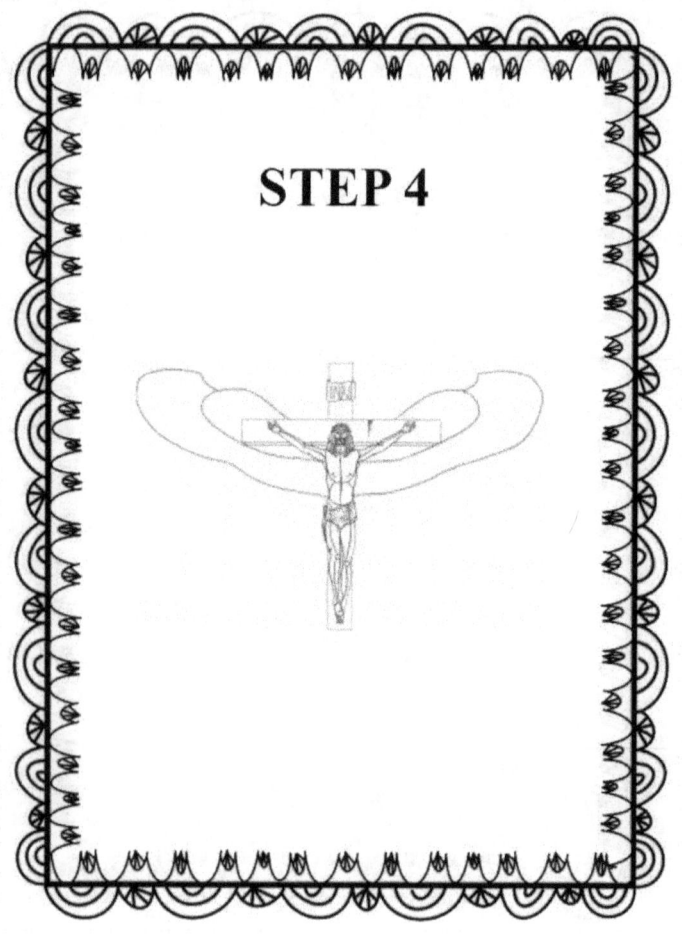

STEP 5

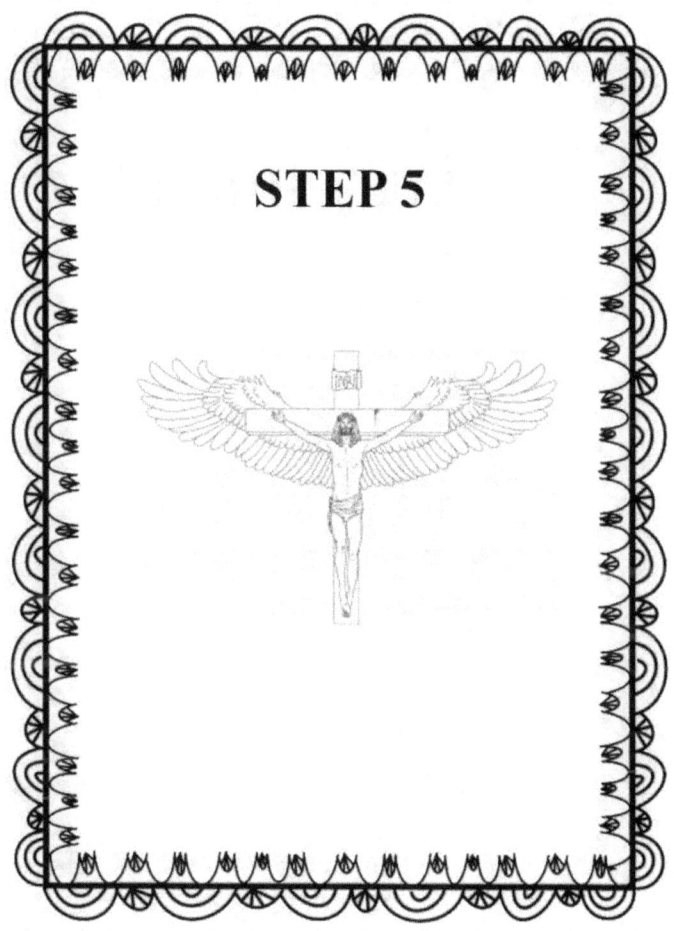

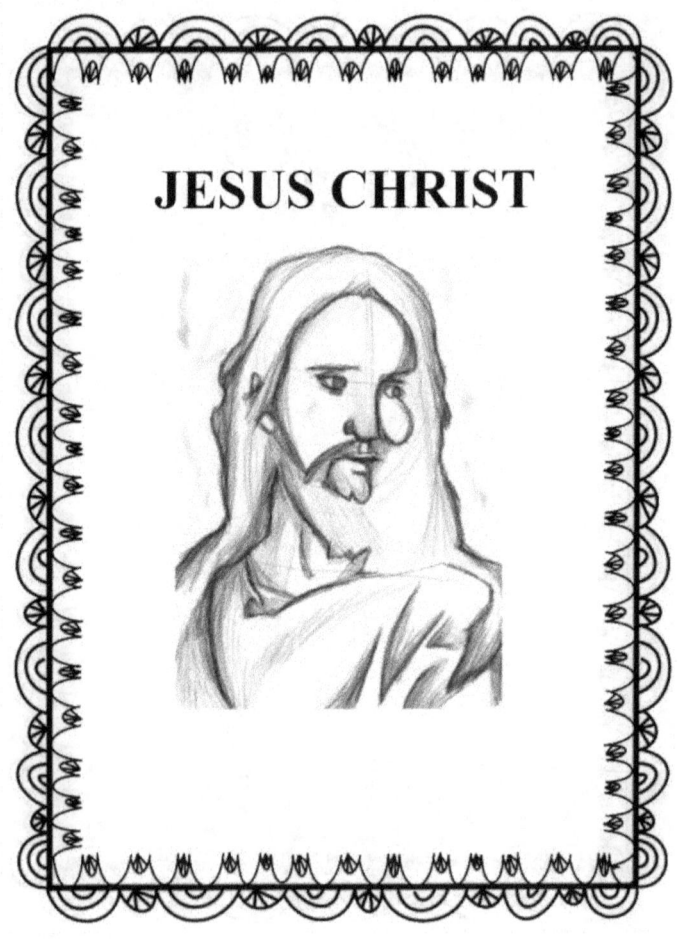

STEP 1

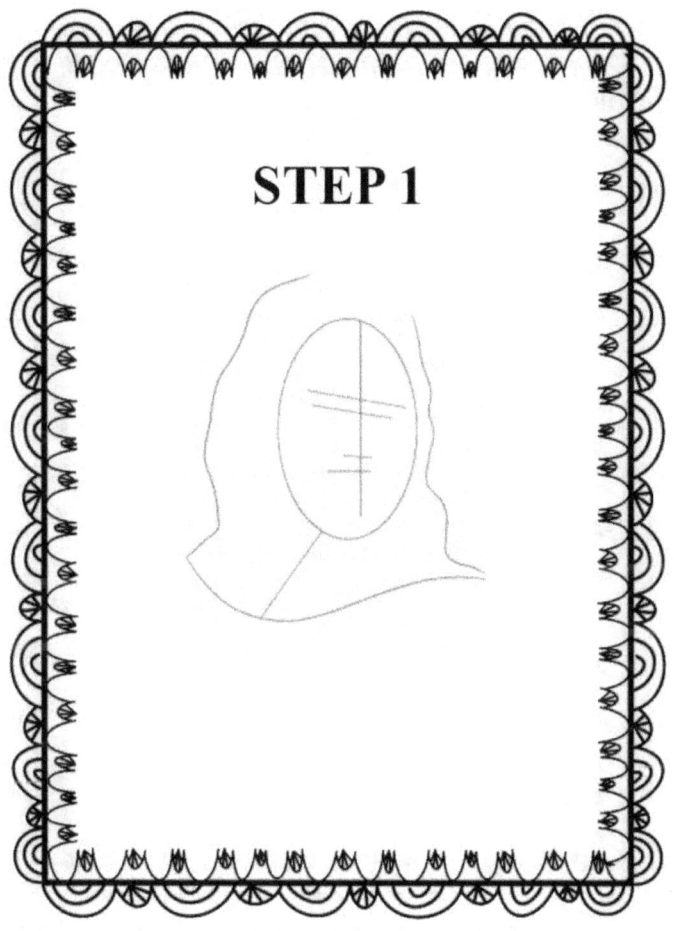

STEP 2

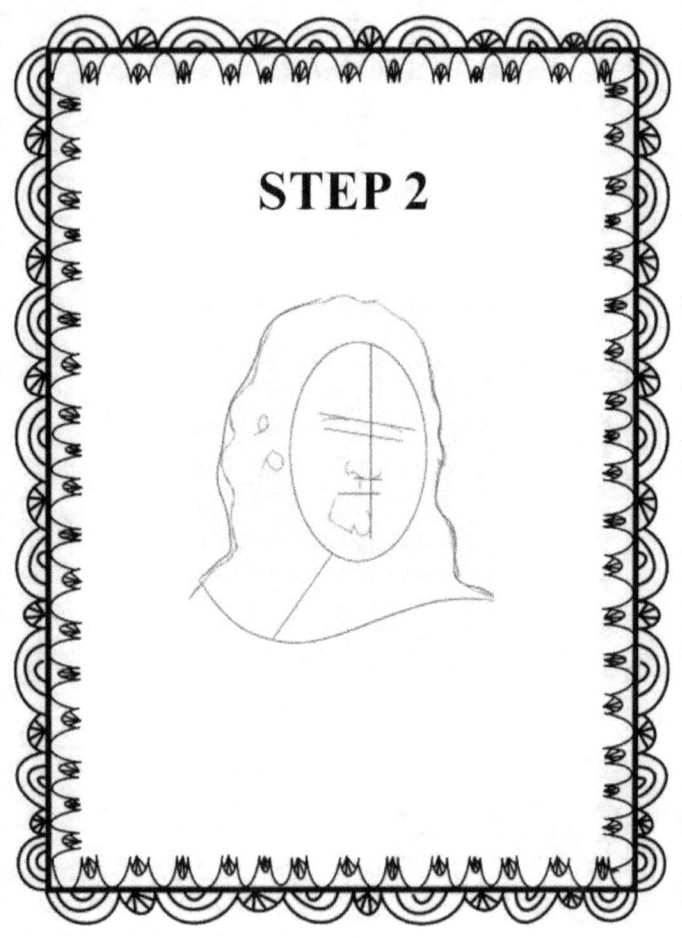

STEP 3

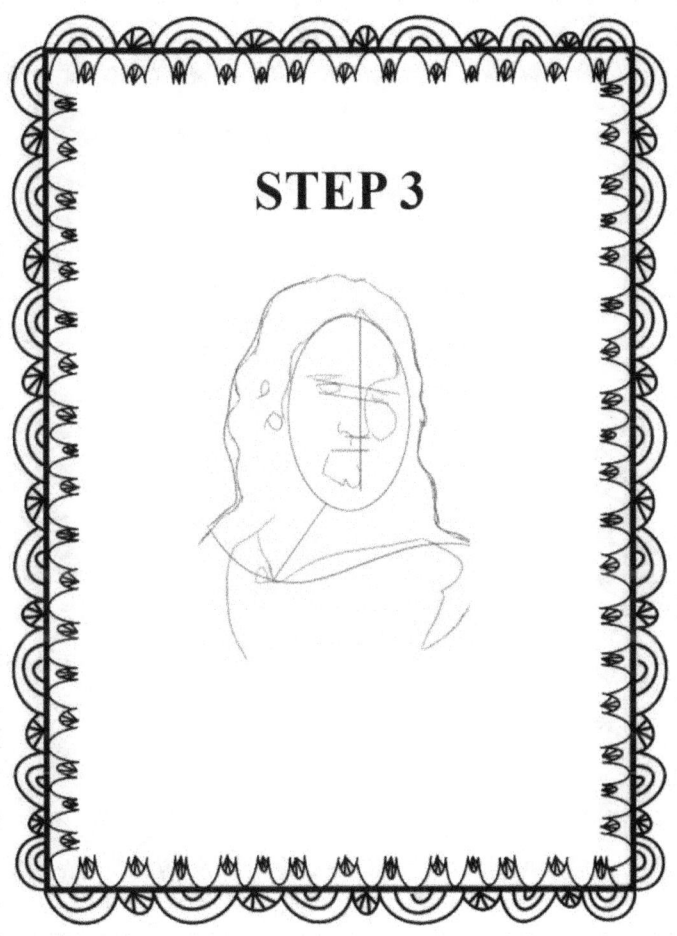

STEP 4

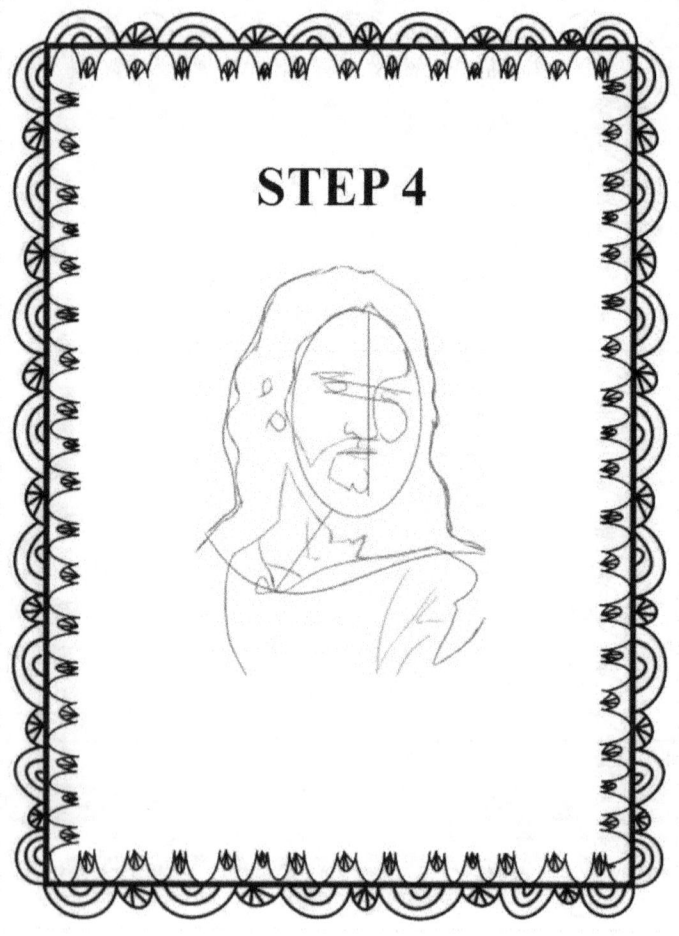

STEP 5

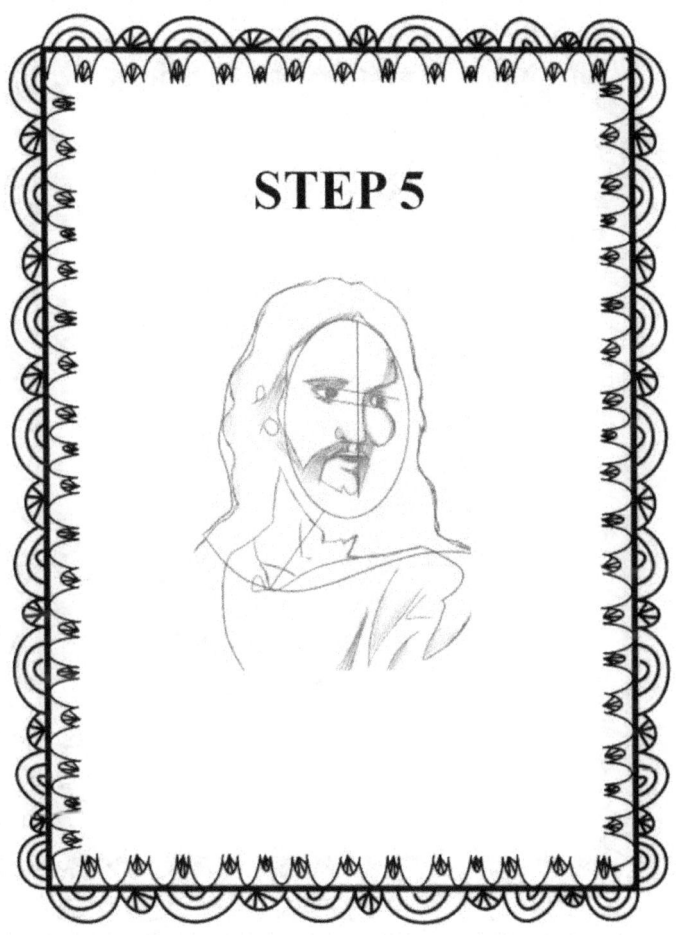

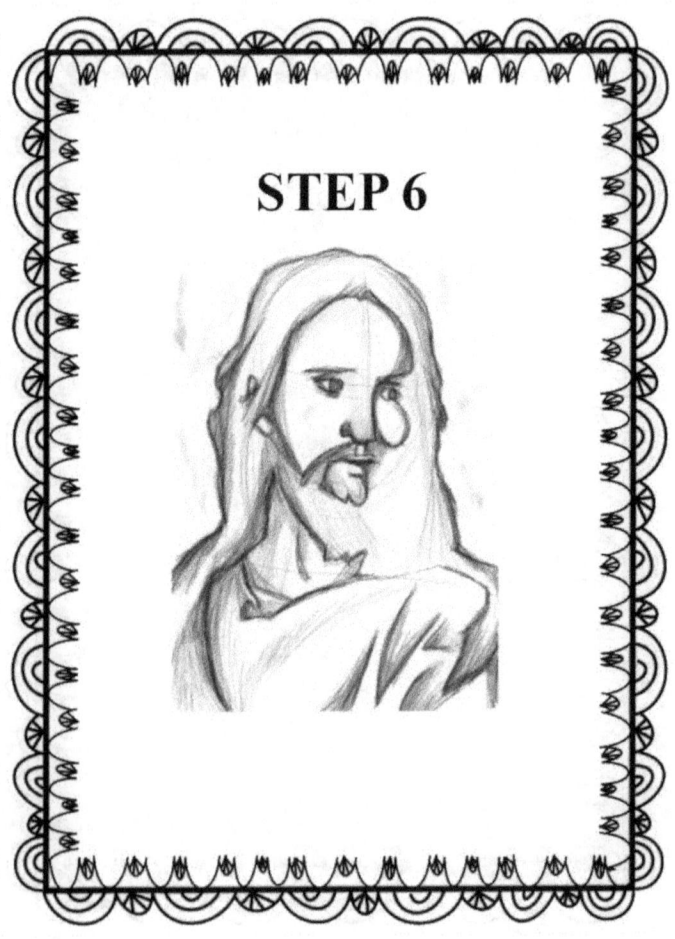

STEP 6

25

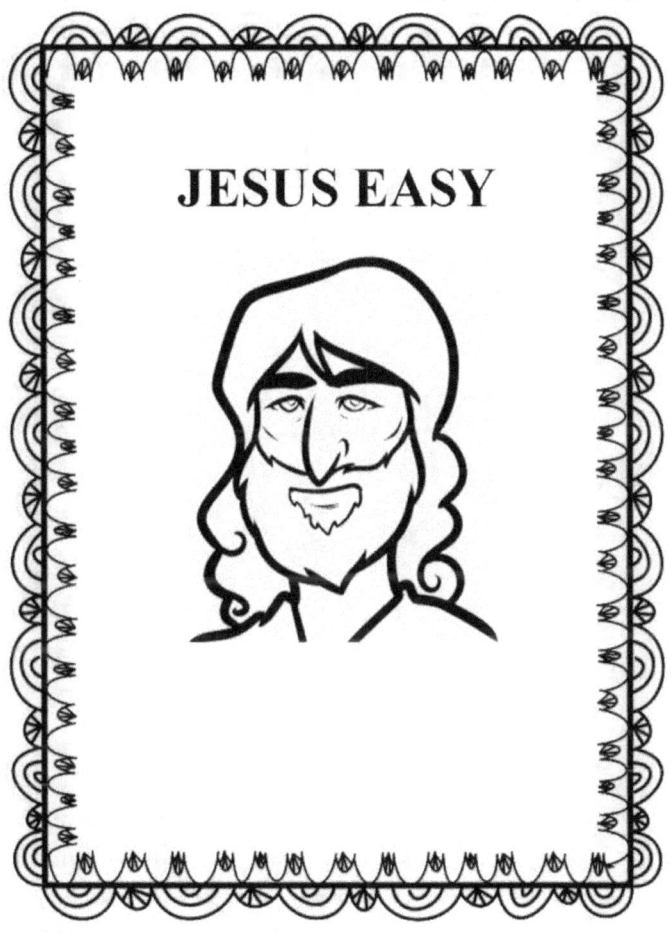

STEP 2

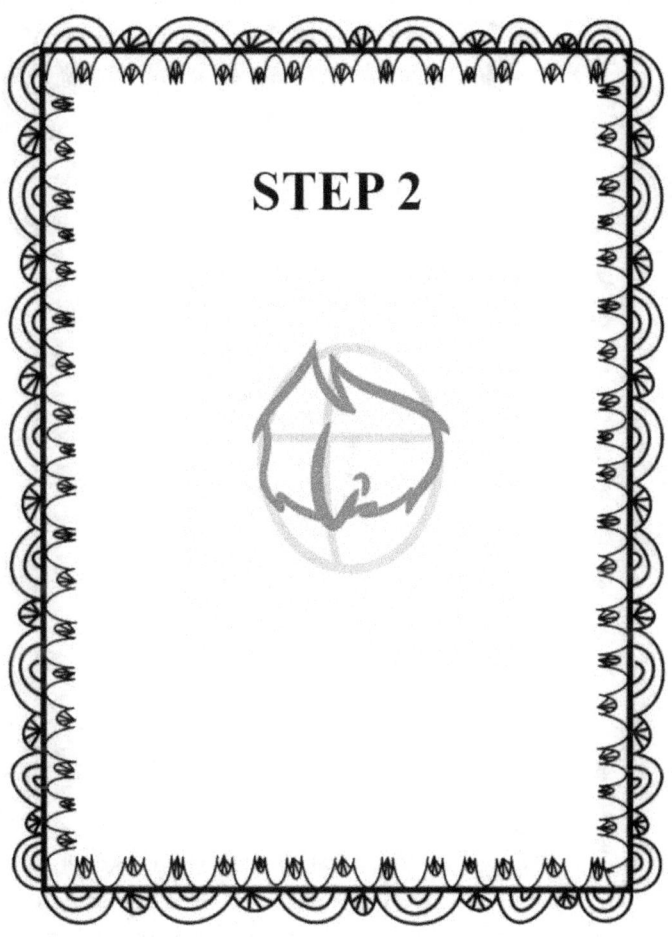

STEP 3

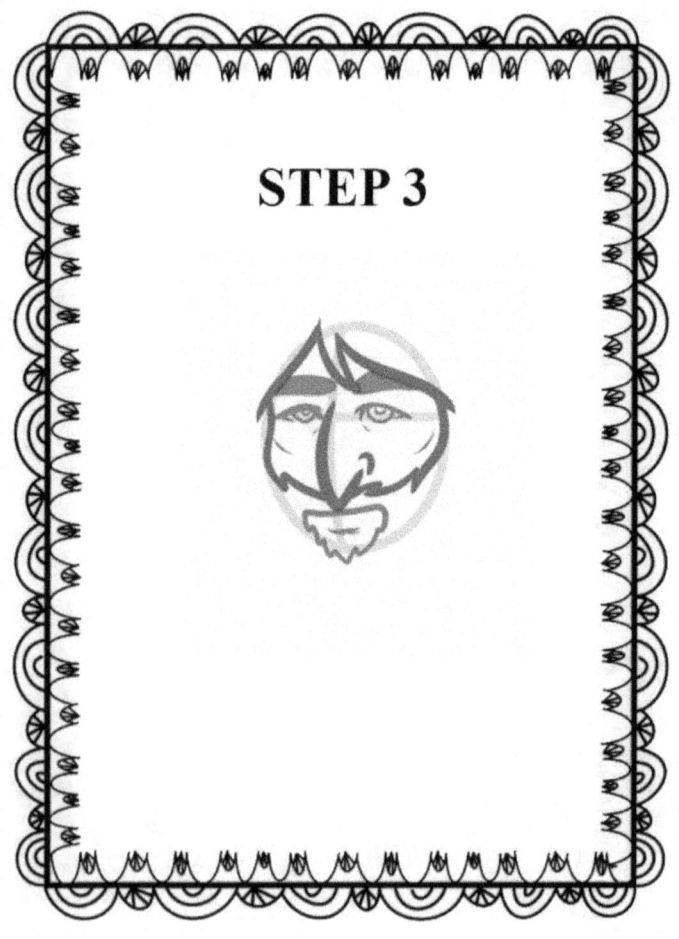

STEP 4

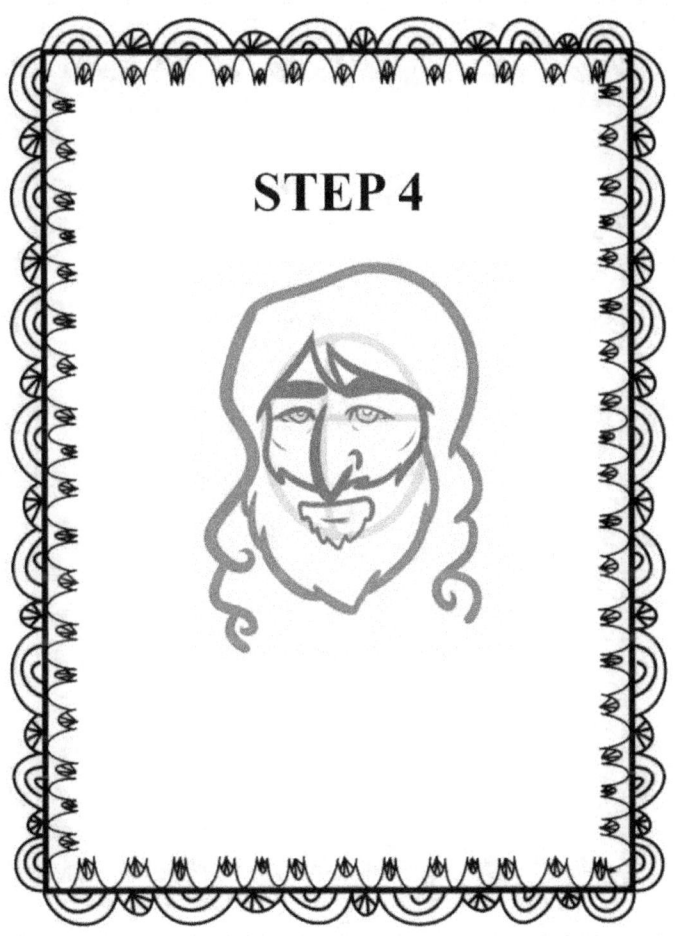

30

STEP 5

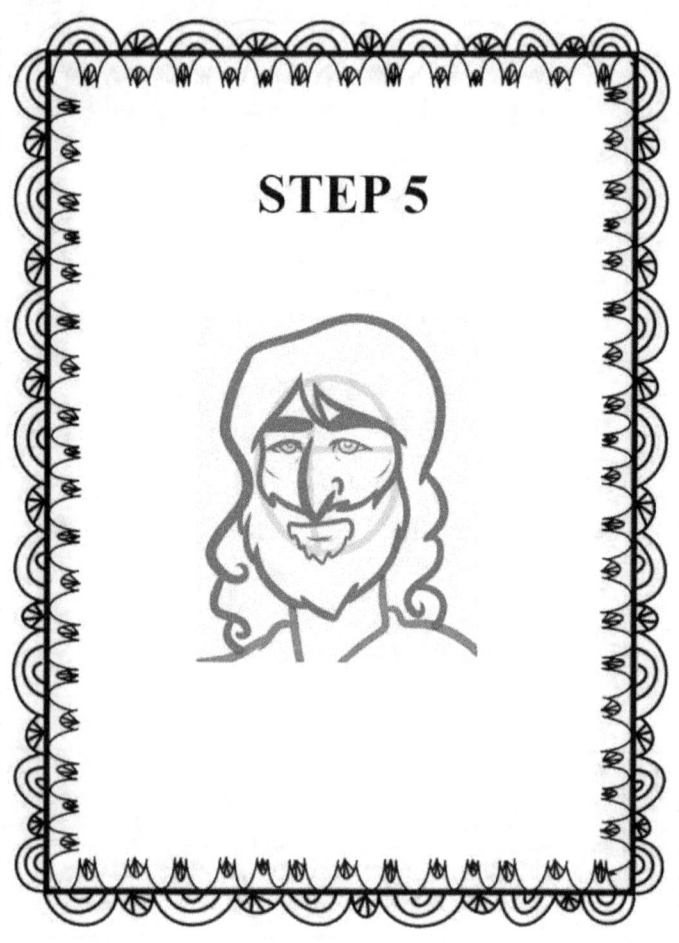

STEP 6

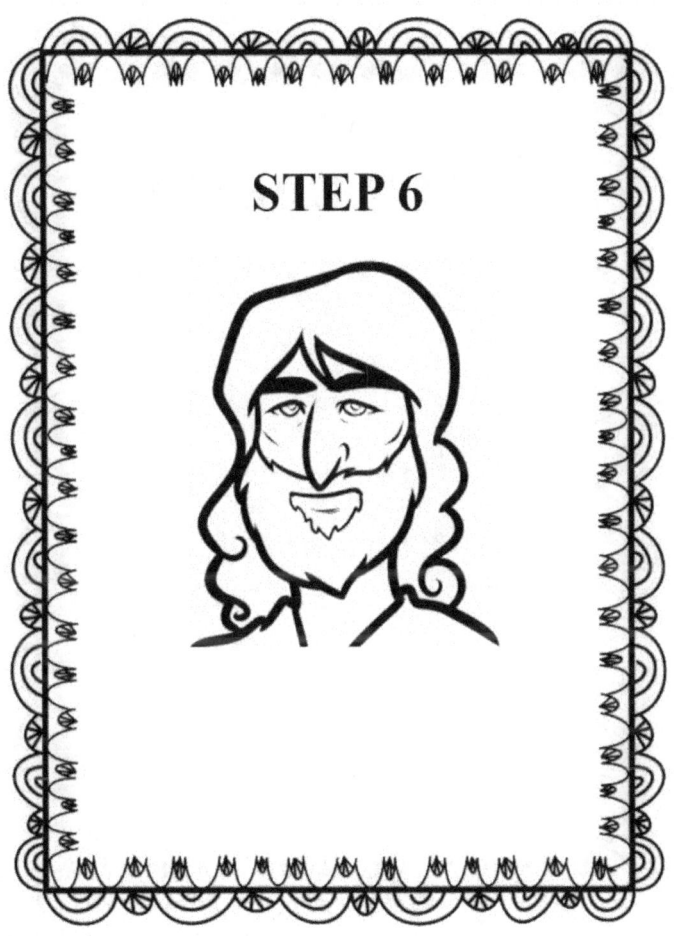

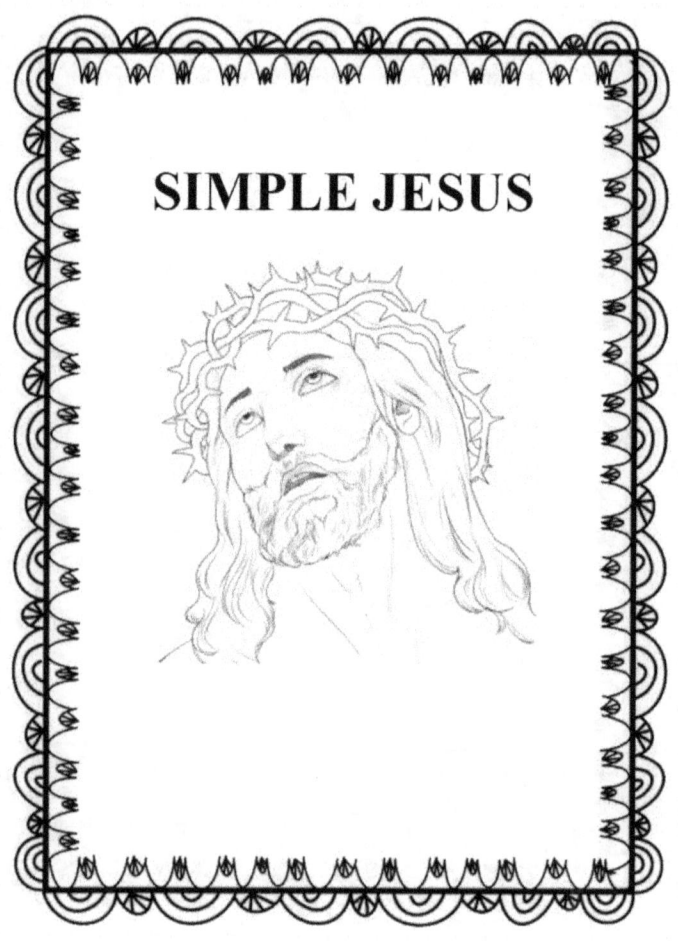

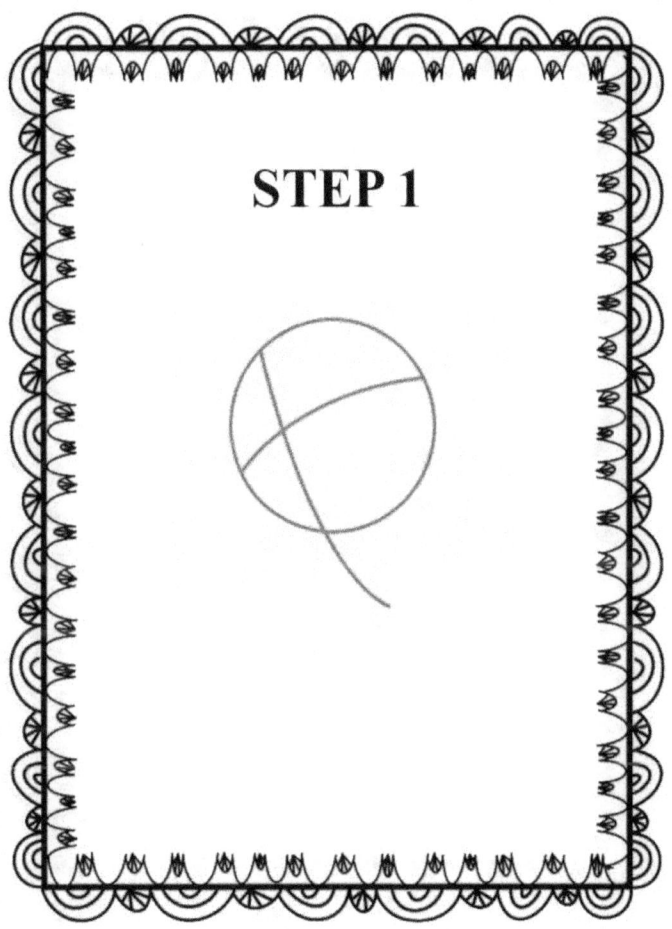

STEP 1

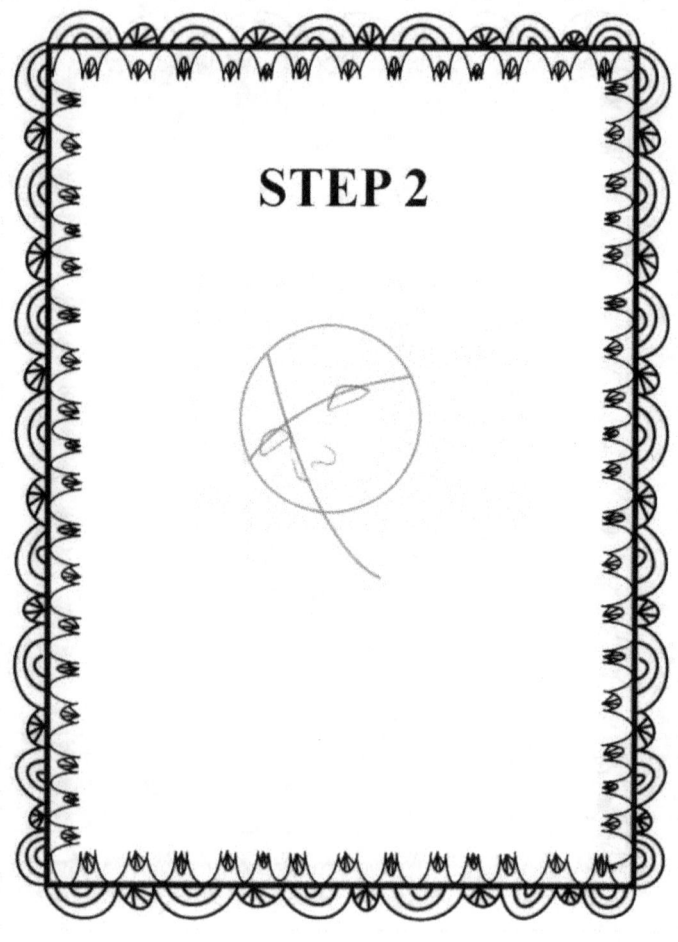

STEP 2

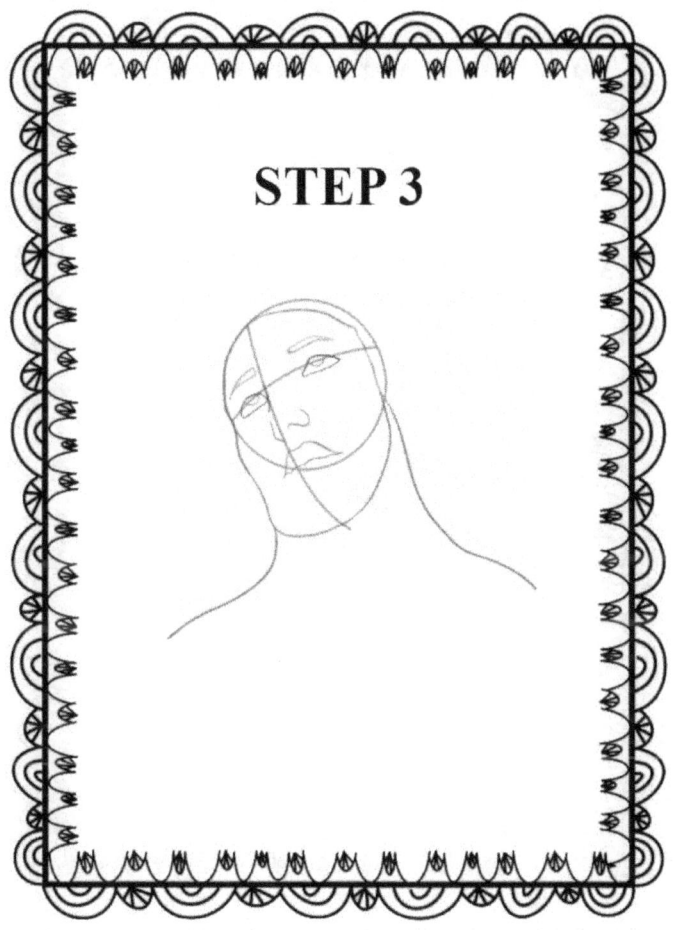

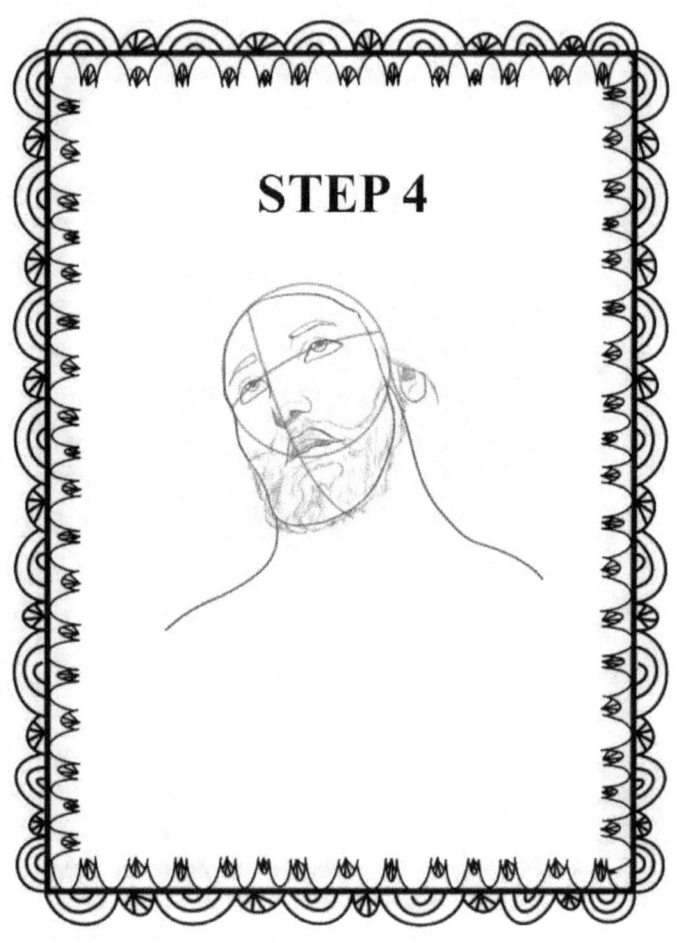

STEP 5

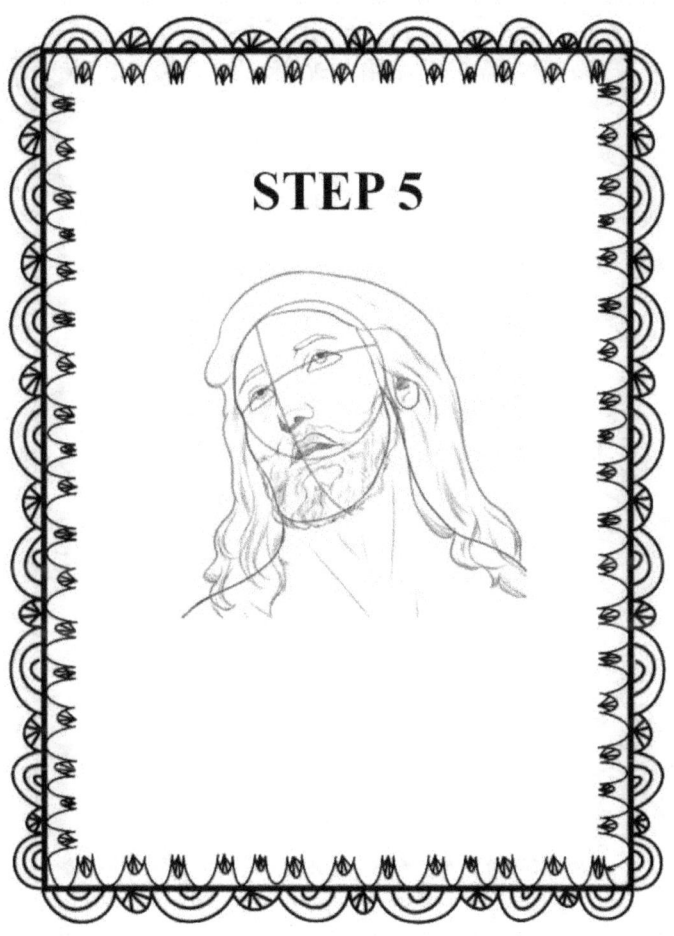

STEP 6

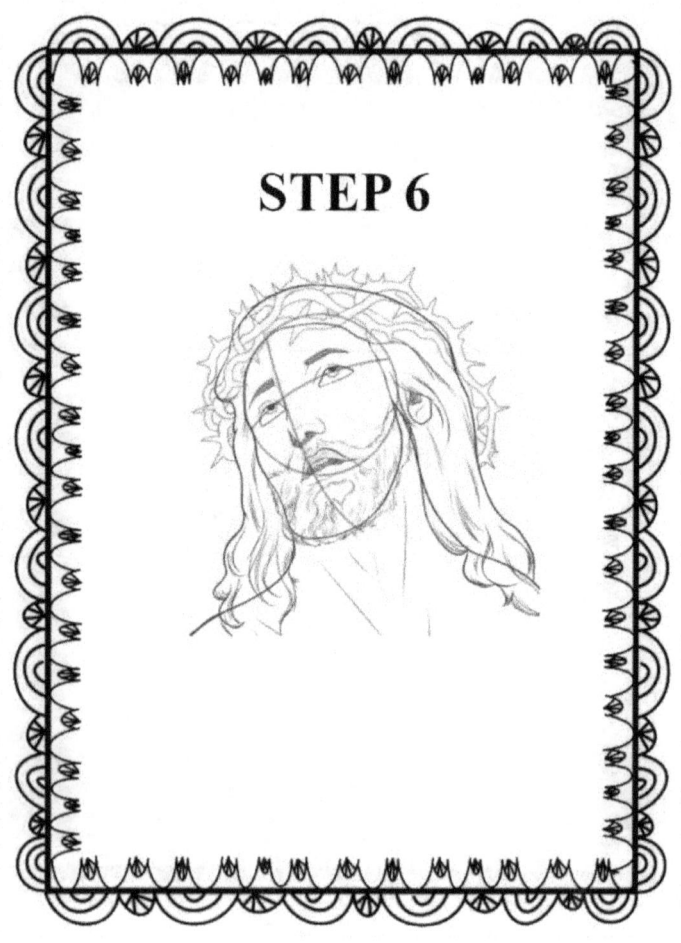

STEP 7

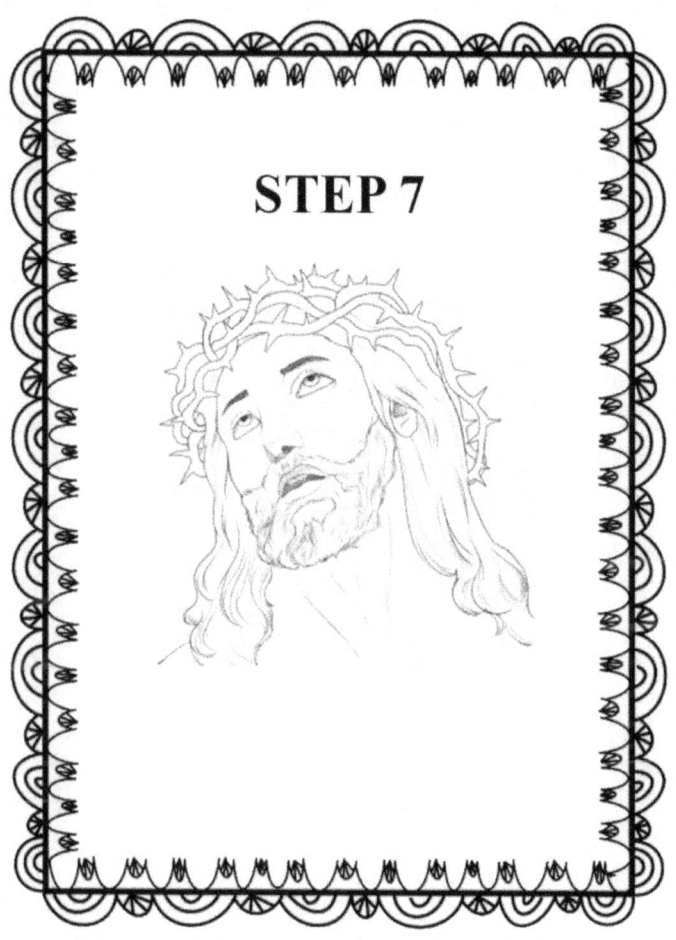

www.ingramcontent.com/pod-product-compliance
Lightning Source LLC
Chambersburg PA
CBHW071550170526
45166CB00004B/1622